Re-story

A Journey of Becoming

Devon Malia Deming

Tehom Center Publishing is a 501(c)3 nonprofit publishing feminist and queer authors, with a commitment to elevate BIPOC writers. Its face and voice is Rev. Dr. Angela Yarber.

Paperback ISBN: 978-1-966655-19-0

Ebook ISBN: 978-1-966655-30-5

In loving memory of
Sharon Sprenger, who always believed in my art,
Hridaya Maling (Little Buddha), who inspired me to see more,
My mom, Candace Ham, who loved Emily Dickinson,
And my dad, Steve Deming, the Cowboy Poet.

May you rest beautifully in the arms of angels!

Contents

SECTION 3: BECOMING

SECTION 1: LIGHT

No Regrets

To say that I regret doing,
Or not doing, anything
In my life would be
To say that I regret
The path
To knowing who I am.

HEART

i remember
in the mist
that night,
wet t-shirt clinging
to my back,
face flushed
with nervous exhaustion,
growing later
with every scurrying second,
and you
in tight black jeans
and standard blazer,
vomiting
in terrified anticipation.
perhaps I did not come
that night for love,
but only to dance
and laugh under the moon.
seventy-two hours
did not pass
between us,
you clutching me
in the moonlight
on your tiny bed.
to die a painful
death you said
would never be too much
and now I have.

STARS

When we were young,
We laid on our backs,
Wet grass on our necks,
Stars watching over us,
Wide eyes filled with wonder.

We did not know then
That our friendship
Would save each other's lives
Over and over again,
Just by being.

CURL

Your smile spreads
In the warm sunlight,
And I feel your face curl
Against my cheek
As you whisper
In my ear

Awake

I lie awake
In the dark —

Feeling you breathe,
Feeling you sleep,
Feeling your skin.

I listen
To the traffic below.
The freight train bellows.
The cat stalks.
The dog snores.
The clock talks,
Tick tick tick ticking
With my heart beat,

Waiting
For that moment
In the grey light
When you reach
for me.

MORNING SONG

In the morning,
I hear you cooking
Through the closed door,

The slow tap of the wooden spoon,
A muffled drum beat backing
Little birds singing
In the yard,

Blending with the notes
Of pots and pans
And the smell of bacon
Sliding under the door.

Visit

When you visit,
You linger,

Dripping down
My body.

When you leave,
All I see is light.

SLEEPLESS

I lie wide-eyed waiting for day,
Thinking of how it will be
When three full moons have traveled
Across this night sky,
Your angelic voice,
Arms longing to hold,
Me longing to be held.

Burning orange crawls
Into the corner of the sky.
I close my eyes and wait
For you.

POUR

Some people exist to pour love out.

Rolling and rollicking

Through every crevice,
Filling empty hearts with light,

Until there is no more darkness.

WANT

I want
A lover
Who wants
To touch my body
And watch it come
Alive,
In awe of the way
Our bodies react
To one another
When we
Want

ETERNITY

How your body

Rises —

In the candlelight
In the moonlight,
In the fading afternoon sun,
With hallelujah music
Playing!

Neither of us have felt
This way
In close to
Eternity.

IDYLLWILD

In Idyllwild, the trees were dying,
But the flowers bloomed
Passionately.

We were there
For no reason
But to be there,

In the quiet of
A mountain breeze,
The crinkle of leaves
Under our feet,
The crackle of a fire
At the foot of our
Small bed,

To be wrapped
In silence,
Together.

Sepia

Those melon hued roses
Will still shine brightly
Even when they have dried
Into sepia memories
Of our wedding day;

Your bare feet in the sand
And a smile beneath
Your freckles,

Reminding me
I still believe
In love.

Apart

In another dimension
Our doppelgängers are barefoot,

Swaying lazily
In a hammock for two,
Sipping tropical cocktails
Under the slippery shade
Of weightless clouds wandering
Over our sun-drenched heads,

In the evening,
We dance in the sand,
Bare hearts under the stars,
And fall perfectly into
Tangled sleep together -

But not here,
In the noise of the city,
Under the weight of work and time,
Our lives live onward,
Miles apart.

Ordinary

Even when our days
Seem simply ordinary
Our moments are gifts

COMING HOME

In this waning evening hour,
The thump of my feet
Echoes over asphalt streets, mingling
With the voices of children
Going home.

On top of my toe, tied keys
Sing to my own home,
Where my longing for you rises and falls
With the curve of piano music, twirling
Over the dusty, dark wood floor
In an empty living room.

I wish
For one life to share with you,
In the twilight of this disappearing day,
To pass the evening on the porch bench
Of one clean house with four dogs,
And children coming home
As the day fades.

WITH ME

You've been with me lately,
In the quiet moments
When my mind wanders off
To another time and place,
Where the sun rises
On the morning horizon,
And I can't quite catch my breath.

PRECIPITATION

i.
It must have been about this time last year,
Rain pouring in torrents from the heavy, weathered
 sky,
You held me tightly against the cold concrete and
 kissed
Me forcefully in the queer light of the storm,
Tiny-fingered rivulets chasing one another down my
 back,
Our long hair wet and clinging to our lips,
Wind chasing the moon.

ii.
At one A.M, the city streets are still.
One car drives up slowly, then speeds away.
I am not afraid.
I hear your voice in the purple night wind,
Your fingertips brush against me in the slow
Drops of rain that linger
In trees and float downward.
I see your face in the stars and know
You will be with me until the sun rises
In the quiet morning, and know
That I am not alone.

iii.
Thirty years ago, they would not have shown her body,
Twisted, mangled, frozen,
On the evening news.
Tonight, her image comes, as if alive,

Into living rooms throughout midwestern states,
A young girl traveling in winter,
Alone,
Dead from fear.

iv.
I leave an empty seat beside me,
As if you were supposed to be
here
In the dark,
In an underground club
In Los Angeles.

I cannot hear the rumbling cadence
Of the rain above
The deep, throaty blonde,
Or the airy brunette,
Or the flute tripping rhythmically over the drums.

Someone says that Jupiter is going to explode,
But we do not know when.

v.
I lie awake, frozen,
Still, even when your hand
Slips softly along my belly
Until we laugh.
Often, I have longed for you
Breathing warmth,
Your nose touching my throat,
But when I feel you,
I cannot raise my eyes,
Rain tapping on the black window,

Red cat screaming at the moon.

vi.
You asked me to speak to you that night
But I could not remember the shapes of words.
I knew only pieces, syllables,
Fragments of imagination.
I knew only that my soul could never belong to you.

Those words echoed unheard off the grey-white ceiling
At three A.M.,
Muffled by rain.

vii.
This year, the water falls continuously,
As if the sky is weeping
For her broken children.
A temblor claims 5,000 human lives
Unexpectedly,
And you are waiting
For something
you cannot name.

viii.
It is useless to know which of our bodies
Will lie down first,
Though your protestations are soundly grounded
In disbelief.
Place my body beneath the soil
To nourish the grass,
To feed the cow,
For they will set my spirit free.

I will come sweetly in the evenings.
I will kiss your sleeping brow.
I will watch over your body in the darkness,
I will watch over you always.

ix.
When the rain ends, I will be standing
In the sunshine, waiting.
I will stand tall under a blue sky,
Face tilted toward
The Mother of Sun,
Mother of Rain,
Eyes raised and palms open,
Bearing gifts of peace and truth,
Which are not mine to give,
Which have always been yours to receive.

x.
At six AM, the city is waking.

One earthworm lies lifeless
In a dirty puddle on the sidewalk.
Others nearby have made it to safety.

Last night, you did not stay with me.
This morning, I rose with the sun.

SECTION 2: DARKNESS

Hell-o

You saying hello
Felt like the devil smiling
In through my peephole

SHIFT

Something inside of you
Shifted
A degree,

Toward fairy tales,
True love,
Happy endings,

And belief,
But then,
It shifted back,

Because you remembered
That you do not

Believe

In magic.

SLID

The days slid
Strangely down
The page
And I felt everything
And nothing
In a single
Elongated
Breath

Beautiful

I felt beautiful once,

Until the pain
Of mistreatment
Filled every crevice
Inside me,

Oozing out
Of my skin,
Swallowing my body whole
And covering
Me.

When you have gone,
I will blossom
Again.

DIN

You cannot live with
The din of your own silence.
Your fear must be loud.

TRACE

I know —
How to walk barefoot
On the floorboards
Without a creak;

How to close a door
Inaudibly with
A silent latch;

How to warm breakfast,
Stopping the oven before
The bell;

How to peel an orange
In one long
Quiet spiral;

How to whisper-scold
The cats climbing the screen
To see the day unfold;

How to make a single
Pot of coffee and clean it,
So it's ready to be made again,

Careful not to replace the empty
Carafe until the plate has cooled
So the glass won't break;

How to wash dishes with a trickle
Of water and replace them
Without a clink;

How to wipe the crumbs
Completely, only leaving
A trace of light;

While she sleeps peacefully.

SIRIUS

Between Sirius
And Venus, I will find rest
With one eye open

SALT

My name is
The Salt Monster,
Because The Crumb Monster
Has already been breathed
Into life
Through
Repeated lore.

My good deeds are invisible,
So no one will know,

And there will never be enough good
To outweigh that speck of salt.

You clean the hot stove behind me
To prove that I am
Worthless
For wanting to let it cool,

So I clean the hot stove,
Even in your absence,
To prove my worth, before
You walk through the door,

Daring to burn
My skin
To erase
Any trace
Of salt.

FORGET

Sometimes I forget
Evil lives under my roof.
Then, I hear her laugh.

Truth

The truth is,
I lied,
When I said
You weren't the reason

For my
       tears,

To protect you
From my sadness,
To protect me
From the truth.

But you have known
The truth all along.

You used my words
Like a knife,
To cut my heart out,

While I watched
It bleed.

STORIES

You will hear stories,

As the gaslighting
Burns the house
Down around us.
Don't believe them.
You will hear —
I am sick,
Mentally ill,
Depressed,
A recluse who hasn't
Left the house in months,
Because she is afraid
Of the world outside;

But I am afraid
Of the anger inside —
The mocking and lies,
The shaming and defaming,
The lack of empathy
From someone I thought
Loved me.
Remember
That you know me,
That you have always
Known me,

And that I am still here
Inside, fighting to get out,
As the flames
Rise.

Unraveling

There were heavy days
When all we could do was watch
The unraveling

Rot

The Universe
Reminds me
That even
The most perfect fruit
Will rot
If not eaten
At just the right
Moment.

CARRY

Sylvia Plath
Gave me a silver jack
And asked me to carry on
What she could not —

To carry the sword,
To carry our songs
To care for them,
To care for me.

For you, I will lift
My words
Above my sorrow
And burn through
The suffering
With the flame
Of your soul on fire.

They blamed
Your blood,
Your becoming,
Your muse,
But not the silent violence
That covered you.

Your words were not
The birth of your despair,
Swallowed by darkness,
But your release.

In them, we will live
Forever.

TEETH

There is no revenge
You can hold tight in your teeth
To find happiness

Remembering

I remember how this part goes —

People choosing you
Because you are bold,

People not understanding me
Because I am quiet,

Not understanding
That years of abuse
Have driven me
Underground
Into silence.

I make myself remember hard
To remind my heart
This silence will not last.

It will fade with the
Fleeting brilliance
Of that costume
You wear,

When your mask
Becomes translucent
In the truth
Of daylight.

Beginnings

I think about
The beginnings —

The first touch,
First dance,
First kiss,

The things people say
When they are falling in love —
From the moment I kissed you
I was making love to you.

I imagine they are true,
At least
They were,

And wonder where
Those feelings go
When life becomes

Ordinary.

BURN

I didn't know the world
Could split open in an instant,
Releasing the ghosts of the past
Into the present,

That years of ugly words
Could split my heart,
Pouring pain over
Hot coals like gasoline,

Or that the only way
To rise from the fire

Is to burn completely to the ground.

Section 3: Becoming

Row

Now is the hard part
When you can't see
The beginnings
From where you came,
And you don't know
Which direction
The winds will blow,

But you must
Put your oars in the water,
Hear the quiet power
Of all those who came before
And all those who will come after,

Chanting together —
Row!

Third Night

On the third night after leaving,
I exhaled cautiously.

Angry messages
Faded into jagged sleep,

With three locks on each door
And three eyes to see.

My breath began to form,
Heart searching for a beat,

But my limbs still cringed
With any disturbance near me.

On the third night of new life,
The third night to be free,

I exhaled, but the inhale
Was yet to come for me.

WEIGHT

You said I had arthritis, too,
Until the doctor said it was
Just fat, but the cat
Jumped up and ran
Across the room

Chasing a ghost,
Or a reflection,
Ten pounds lighter, almost.
Sometimes, you need to
Let go

Of unnecessary weight
To gallop toward
The light, instead of letting
Strangers' chaos weigh
You down.

On any day in my future history,
I'd rather that my love be judged
On Rumi's scales
Than for my sleeve to bleed
Unnecessarily.

TOLL

What will it cost
To unbury my soul?

The bruises at most
Are still healing,
At best,
Reliving my history
The burden of being,
Retelling my story
And changing its meaning.

It will cost you
An ear,
A scar, a heart,
A toll of telling,
Of fear
And grieving,

Wringing hands, salty eyes,
Prayers in the dark,
No room for lies, lying
Still in the quiet.

You will pay in treasure
To unbury me.

SEE THEM

You
Feel alone
Like the only one
Who ever walked this path,
But look closer
And you will see them,
The well-worn footprints
Of thousands of others
Who share your story,
All standing beside you,
Lifting you up
And pulling
You forward.

CELEBRATION

When I turned 49,
I baked a cake for me.
I decorated it painstakingly,
With a message of love
From me to me,
In rainbow colored icing
To celebrate silver linings
This year unfolded so
Unexpectedly.

The rejoining of a torn birth cord,
New stories from a history unseen,
The evening that we talked of death,
Or near death, I learned
That she had floated peacefully
Above us on the day I was born
And been given the choice to stay
Or leave.

How could I leave she asked
When you were just breathing?

Thank you for coming back
For me.

COMING BACK TO LIFE

The tears have been enough
To melt away a whole body,
An entire lifetime of moments
That became too heavy to hold
In two small arms,

But this sun keeps rising,
Timid pink in the first light of morning,
Then growing so bright
You can't look at it
Without squinting back the tears.

It does not stop
Giving,
Burning,
Growing,
Living,
Loving,

Even after the tears are gone.

Feel

Yesterday,
I woke up smiling,
Laughed in my pillow,
Cried tears of joy,

Cried tears of sorrow,
Ate cookies for breakfast,
Celebrated best friends,

Shared coffee,
Shared time,
Made plans,

Embraced love,
Radiated pride,
Cherished joy,

Honored gratitude,

Shared spirits,
Savored wine,
Sang and danced,

Laughed more,

Held hands,
Held hearts,
Held on,

Felt peace.

Today,
I cannot remember
How to feel.

EGGSHELL

I surround myself with blue
For comfort —

An antique eggshell vase,
With indigo daisies
Hiding a peeking bluebird
And a butterfly with
Jeweled wings,

A flickering candle
With the scent of sea
Calling me back to
My ocean home,

And a simple
Welcoming sofa
The color of lazy waves
To hold my head
And my dreams.

Pure Love

To care for me like you
Care for me,
Pure love with orange rays of light,
You lift me over your shoulders
To see

You
Standing up for me,
Standing beside me,
Standing with me,
Standing behind me,

Your strong hands
Speaking truth
With outstretched arms,
In love, wrapped tight.

To care for me like you
Care for me

Will make me
Strong
And loved

Unconditionally.

WISDOM

You asked if I was born
With wisdom in my mouth
And I laughed,
Releasing my confessions
Carefully into the the air
Between us.

You know the truth —
That wisdom
Is only birthed
Through suffering,

That these swords
Can be my cage,
Or my protector,
Or the iron that drives me,

If I open my eyes
Wider
Instead of
Wishing.

And that the hardest choice
Is to open the door
To let the light in
Before you are ready
To be seen.

I Can

I can —

Wake up in the morning
Under a soft blanket,
Bright sun through the
Window giggling;

Meander toward the kitchen
To savor my own cup
Of strong coffee brewing,
With birds singing;

Wash vegetables
From a local garden,
To keep me healthy,
And shining;

Stroll in the afternoon breeze
Through sheltering trees,
With dancing flowers
And children laughing;

Laugh, cry
Think, speak
Read, write
Play, Sing

Breathe.

ENOUGH

I never felt you
In that slow dance
At my conservative cousin's wedding,
Or in any other.

Two women embracing,
Moving silently over the parquet wood,
With two hundred eyes
Watching loudly.

I know that I will have
The joy in my heart again
To dance without
Judgement,
Or anger,
Or fear;

To feel my partner's love
In a glance,
In a touch,
In a breath;

Gliding over the floor
In unity,
Praising love,
And we will be

Enough.

Rainbow

In the darkest times
There are rainbow paths that lead
Out of suffering

VINES

Under angels' shadows cast,
I lose my mind
In the ocean, vast and blue,

Where I forget
Stories repeating,
Like reading your lips,

Like how you see Jesus
In my forehead, in the discolor
Of my skin, that tells another

Story within, of age, not beauty —
Not age, but beauty —
One cannot be pulled from the other,

Like how the words change
As they grow from your mouth,
From poisonous vines

Into flowers of forgiveness.

Peace

Peace comes
Unexpectedly,

Taps you on the shoulder
In the middle of the night,

Startles you awake,
Smiling from a dream,
To whisper in your ear —

This is life.
This will pass,
And you will be okay.

STILL

This plain white cotton pillowcase does not wear
The lingering indentation of your forehead in the
    morning
Or the sweet scent of your skin at midnight.

Still, I have found peace on this island,
In memories of sleepy Sundays,
Slow-dancing in the crackling dark of your living room
Lit only by the fire,
The mischievous curve of your smile
Beneath dark lashes tickling my cheek.

These pictures will carry me on their backs
To where the ripened fruit falls effortlessly at my feet.

Through the open window of my father's car
Traveling south on Crenshaw Boulevard,
The scent of summer in your backyard beckons
To me on the wind.

CROWN

They see

A jeweled crown,
A wrinkled nose,
A crooked confident smile,
A pretty girl standing tall.

I am broken
But my tattered wings
Are strong enough
To fly.

BREATHING

In the dark, I trace the stars,
Awake with moving pictures

Of goddesses, animals, and figures
Guiding me through the night.

Each wave that breaks
Outside my window is a breath —

Reminding me to exhale,
Reminding me to inhale,

Breathing out the fear,
Breathing in the learning.

My breathing meets the ocean's
To make peace,

Making peace with my past,
Making peace within me,

Above the snoring
Of two happy cats at my feet.

Second Chances

The Earth speaks in ways
That people cannot -
In rainclouds followed rainbows,
In stars dancing with sun and moon,
In wind pushing waves
Toward the safety of the shore,
In flowers reaching up
To embrace the sun.

Today, lines of clouds
Streak across the sky,
A lion's mane flowing,
The king racing over the plain.

They rise up from the Earth,
Out over the ocean,
Ashes from lost bodies floating,
Flying, 600,000 souls moving on.

I lie with my back,
On the soft grass of the bluff,
Suspended between clouds and waves,
Honoring the grey mourning
With a celebration of living,
Grieving the losses
And grateful for second chances.

AFTER

Before you know it,
The rain has passed,
And you blink, blinded
By streams of sparkling sunshine
Pushing through your
Half-closed lashes.

You dodge slow moving
Elephant tear drops,
Falling unexpectedly,

The final remnants
Of the storm
Clinging to leaves.

ALIVE

Venus was keeping me
Alive last August,
When sleep did not

Come easily
In the corner
Of one room.

Tonight,
She sings
Of Freedom.

PINK

Pink is the color of
Ripe grapefruit in the morning
And guava on
A Hawaiian lanai,
Dripping;

The mane of a unicorn,
The wig of a queen,
Feathered lashes
That match my boa,
And a tattoo with wings;

The pop of a celebration,
Glow of love's blush,
Hands held high,
Parades colored bright,
And confetti slowly streaming;

A gentle blossom's breath,
Uniquely unfurling,
The sweet sensitivity
Of a morning flower,
With lips serene;

The brush of eternity,
A touch of magic
Unconditional love,
From my deepest heart,
Overflowing;

A bold sunrise,
A quiet sunset,
And the promise
That each day
New opportunity brings.

FEARLESS

This heart has been broken
And carefully pieced back
Together so many times
That it is fearless.

I will bring you my best,
Because any less
Would not be living
Courageously.

INVISIBLE

Such a small thing, kindness — Yet,
Slippery, like the silver that shimmers
On breaking waves.

You cannot hold it carefully in your hand,
Capture it in a perfect picture,
Or tie it delightfully in a pretty box.

It is invisible as the heart,
Only seen in soulful eyes or felt
In a thoughtful, tender touch.

Kindness is the hidden treasure,
That once unburied,
Connects us in its glow.

GIFTS

You gave me
Honesty and freedom.
You broke
My fall.

You awakened
Sleeping Sappho
And unhinged
Her mouth.

You gave me
Inspiration, and encouragement,
Laughter,
A song,

The power to heal others'
Wounds with words,
And slow days to
Find my heart.

How could I not

Let you go
With love?

WITH GRACE

When we had walked
A little farther
Down the lane together,

She knelt to pick a flower,
Turned to me with shiny eyes
And asked,

Am I the only one who is afraid?
No, I answered softly

We will carry one another's
Trembling hearts

With grace.

SMILE

I cannot force this smile
Into submission,
To keep it from crawling quietly
Across my face,
Knowing how deeply I am loved.

ACKNOWLEDGMENTS

This collection is over thirty years in the making, as many of these poems were written in my college days at the University of California, Los Angeles, in the early 1990's and their breadth spans more than three decades up to the present. Thank you to every teacher, reader, friend, and partner who inspired them and received them along the way.

To the readers that helped shape the individual poems chosen for this collection - Mandy, Tanya, Hilary, Courtney, Caron, Jackie, Linda, and Sharon - thank you for your gift of time and loving feedback! Alida, Sally, Wendy, and Tova, thank you for your deeper dive and final edits!

Thank you to Austyn Wells and Dr. Maria Furlano, both spiritual teachers and mentors who created a safe space for my creativity to flow and evolve into a beautiful energy of its own, and to Alida Thacher and the Thursday afternoon writing group for inspiring me to keep creating.

To my soul sisters, AWSMU family, Art of Tuning In Studio members, and my besties, thank you for continuing to light the way forward and row in my boat!

And to Dr. Angela Yarber and Tehom Center Publishing, thank you for believing this book will find its place in the world and continue to inspire others.

All of my love,
Devon

ALSO BY DEVON MALIA DEMING

Previously Published Poems in this Collection

"Enough", *Slamming Bricks: An Anthology 2nd Edition*, September 2022 (https://www.blurb.com/b/11267760-slamming-bricks-an-anthology-2nd-edition)

"heart", *oddball magazine*, September 2021 (https://oddballmagazine.com/poem-by-devon-deming/)

"Pink", *Vocal Media*, May 2021(https://vocal.media/poets/pink-vqmdf0x2r)

"Sirius", *Vocal Media,* January 2023 (https://vocal.media/poets/what-will-you-inspire)

"Vines", oddball magazine, October 2021. (https://oddballmagazine.com/poem-by-devon-deming-2/)

Other Published Poems

"Arms of Angels", *Pure Messengers: Angel Poems,* March 2023 (https://lelivros.shop/pure-messengers-angel-poems-english-edition)

"Collections", *Prometheus Dreaming,* Thus Spake Prometheus Featured Poem of the Month September 2021 (https://www.youtube.com/watch?v=i82SzAMAiso)

"Disturbed", *Slamming Bricks: An Anthology 3rd Edition,* August 2023 (https://www.blurb.com/b/11675349-slamming-bricks-an-anthology-3rd-edition)

"Fading", *Vocal Media*, January 2023, (https://vocal.media/poets/fading-om6pnc04r9)

"Family", *Slamming Bricks: An Anthology 2nd Edition,*

September 2022 (https://www.blurb.com/b/11267760-slam ming-bricks-an-anthology-2nd-edition)

"Home", *Vocal Media*, September 2021, (https://vocal.media/poets/home-36rzge01wd)

"Love Like Ocean Flows: Four Water Haikus", *Vocal Media*, January 2023 (https://vocal.media/poets/love-like-ocean-flows)

"Seen", *Slamming Bricks: An Anthology 3rd Edition,* August 2023 (https://www.blurb.com/b/11675349-slamming-bricks-an-anthology-3rd-edition)

"Soul", *Vocal Media*, January 2023, (https://vocal.media/poets/soul-w2hh0yrs)

Other Published Works

"Broken Pictures" (Short Story), *Vocal Media*, March 2022 (https://vocal.media/families/broken-pictures)

"Vanpooling and Its Effect on Commuter Stress" (Co-Author), *Research in Transportation Business & Management*, November 2018 (https://www.researchgate.net/publication/328989927_Vanpooling_and_its_effect_on_commuter_stress)

"Exploring Airport Employee Commute and Parking Strategies" (Topic Panel/Contributing Author), *Airport Cooperative Research Program (ACRP) Synthesis 36, National Academies of Sciences, Engineering and Medicine*, 2012 (https://nap.nationala cademies.org/read/22724/chapter/1)

"College Student Transit Pass Programs", *Transit Cooperative Research Program (TCRP) Synthesis 131, National Academies of Sciences, Engineering and Medicine*, 2018 (https://nap.nationala cademies.org/read/25052/chapter/1)

www.devonmaliademing.com